eye v
meat-eat

fickfock MEDIA

Think...

Do they have mouths?

How do they trap their prey?

How do they eat?

All plants need light from the sun, water from the soil and carbon dioxide from the air in order to grow. But some plants grow in places with poor soil – in deserts, on mountainsides or even on the branches of rainforest trees. These plants supplement their diet with juicy, nutrient-rich bugs! They actually eat meat! These plants are called carnivorous plants.

Imagine...

If you were a bug, would you fall into their trap?

It looks like you are about to find out...

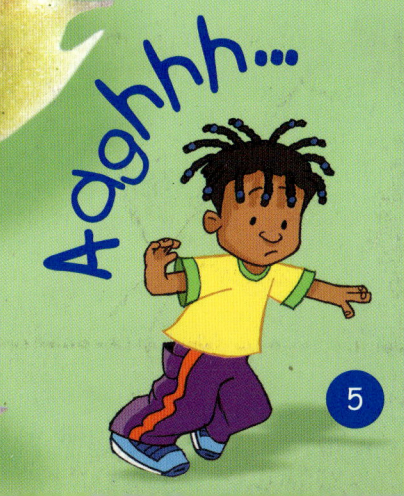

Aaghhh...

This is a pitcher plant

These plants live in the bogs and swamps of America. They are sometimes called North American pitcher plants.

The inside of the plant is very slippery. Any bug that climbs in will lose its grip on the surface and... fall down!

Can you see the tiny hairs that grow on the lid of the plant? They help the bugs hang on...briefly!

Bugs are attracted to the bright colours and sugary nectar on the lid of the plant.

I'm going to fall...

These pitchers sleep during the winter when there are no bugs to eat. They go brown and die down, coming to life again in the spring.

These plants have digestive juices (like you have in your stomach) at the bottom of their long stems. When a bug falls down into the juice it dissolves, and its goodness is soaked up by the plant.

This is a venus fly trap

The traps snap shut as fast as I can clap.

Venus fly traps are the best known carnivorous plants. Like some other meat-eating plants, they actually move to catch their prey.

The bright colour of the mouth of the trap lures bugs inside.

There are tiny hairs on the inside of the mouth. The slightest touch of these hairs will cause the trap to shut.

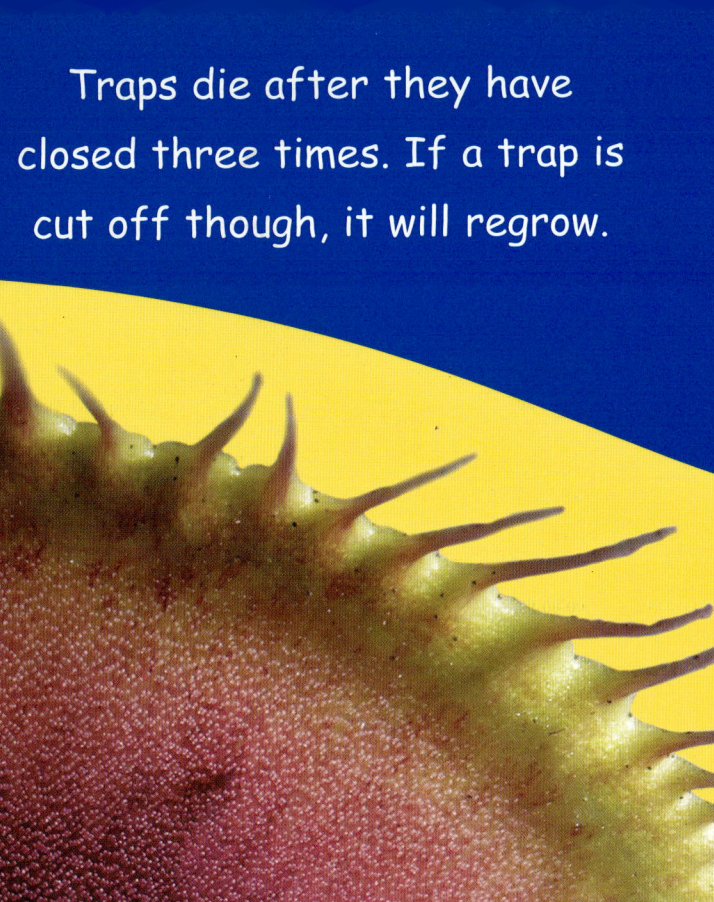

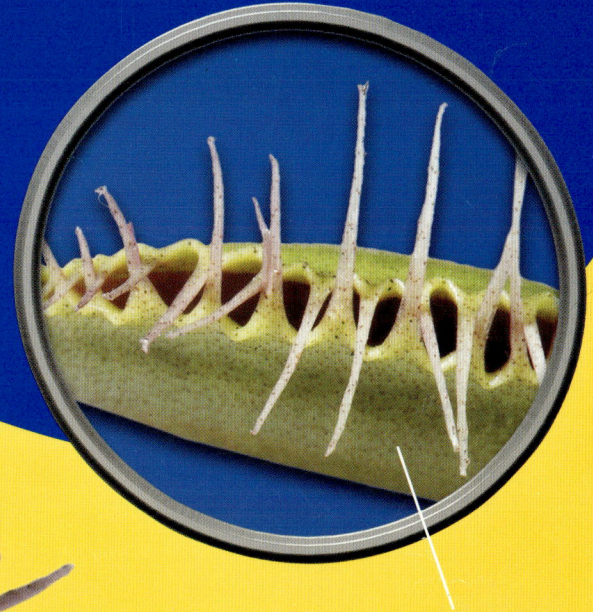

Traps die after they have closed three times. If a trap is cut off though, it will regrow.

The teeth on the edge of the trap close so tightly that a bug cannot break free.

When the trap is shut, the plant releases its digestive juices and absorbs all the goodness in the bug, leaving just a dry shell.

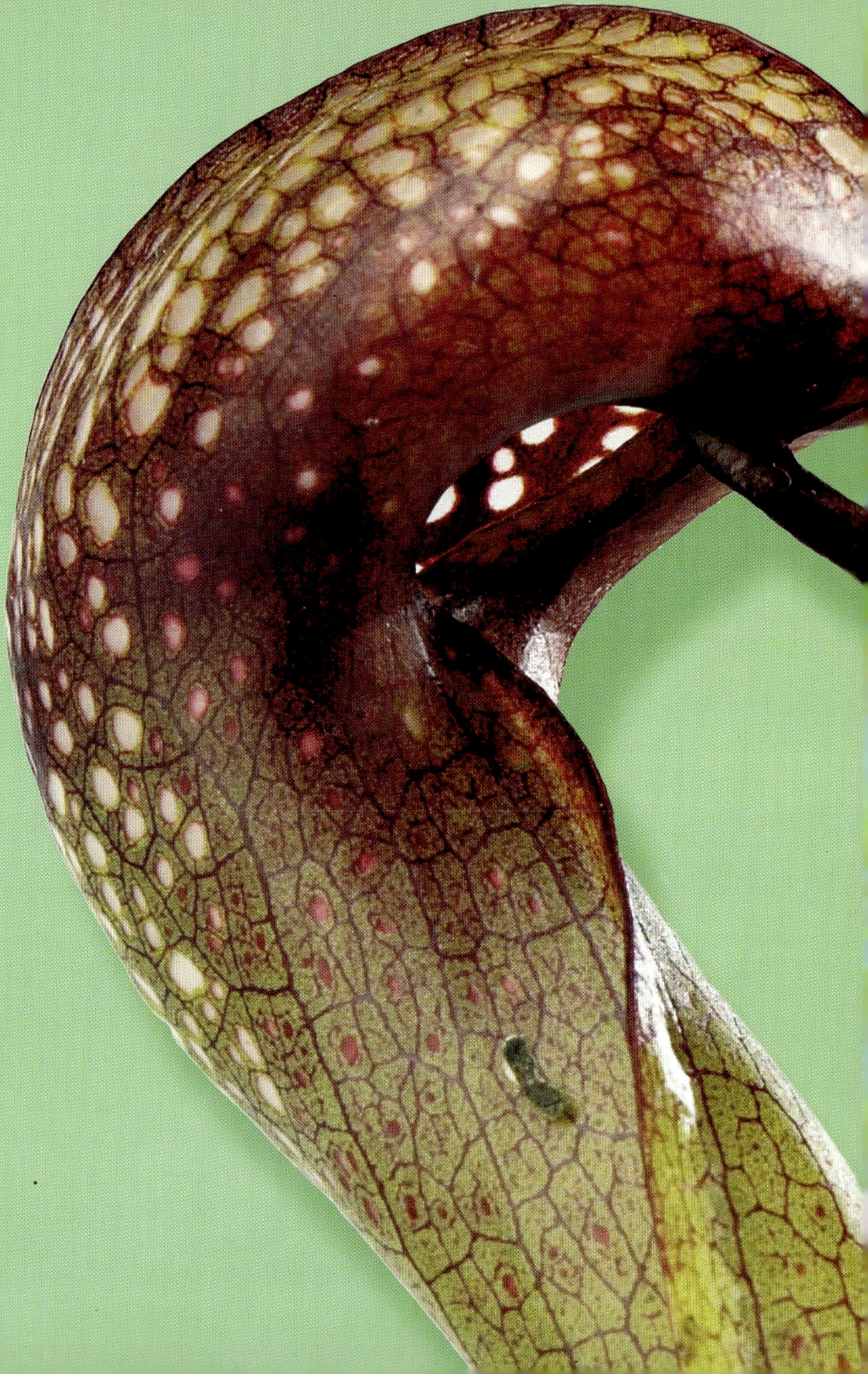

Aaghh...
is this a snake?

The trapped bug flies at the windows again and again, soon becoming confused.

There are tiny windows in the roof of the trap that make the bug think it's a way out!

Once inside, a fringe of hairs forces the bug towards the back of the trap, where the surface is dangerously slippery...

Waiting for the bug at the bottom of the neck is a pool of water and digestive juice.

no, it's a cobra lily

These plants look like cobra snakes and are just as deadly to bugs!

The Trap

Cobra lilies can live in mountain bogs as high up as 2,500 metres!

Their fang-like leaves act as landing pads for bugs, which are attracted to the bright pink colour and sweet taste. The bug lands and is tempted inside the trap.

this is a sun pitcher

It is only found on the top of Angel Falls in South America. This plant has a nectar spoon.

Bugs lose their balance on the slippery nectar spoon and fall down through the plant.

It's like falling down a well!

The sun pitcher eats the trapped bugs by attacking them with bacteria.

The red colouring on a sun pitcher increases when the plant gets a lot of sunlight.

This plant is bright and sugary – good enough to eat!

Each horn is really a leaf that has wrapped round and joined together to make a trap for unsuspecting bugs!

is this a monster...

16

...with jaws?!

no it's just a small albany pitcher

Albany pitchers are found in boggy, grassy areas of Australia.

The sharp teeth surround the opening of the trap, making it impossible for a bug to escape after it has fallen in!

The lid of the trap.

Once a bug is inside the trap, it loses its grip on the surface and falls into a pool of digestive juices.

Albany pitchers have hairs on the outside of the trap. They are used to guide bugs inside where they will be attracted by the nectar on the walls.

The albany pitcher's traps look a bit like baby boots.

The lid of the trap can close to protect the digestive juices from drying up in hot weather.

Albany pitchers are not very big. They grow to a maximum of 4 centimetres in length.

this is a monkey cup

Monkey cups grow on trees in the tropical rainforests of Southeast Asia.

Each cup has special areas around the lid which give off nectar, attracting bugs – and sometimes small animals as well.

Bugs are also attracted to the bright pink colour of the lid.

The bugs and other tiny creatures fall down into the cup and are dissolved by the digestive juices in the bottom.

The monkey cups are really the plant's traps, but like most carnivorous plants, these traps don't actually close.

These spikes along the side of the monkey cup also help to trap bugs.

Monkeys have been seen using the cups to drink from!

22

YIKES,
it's like a jungle in here!

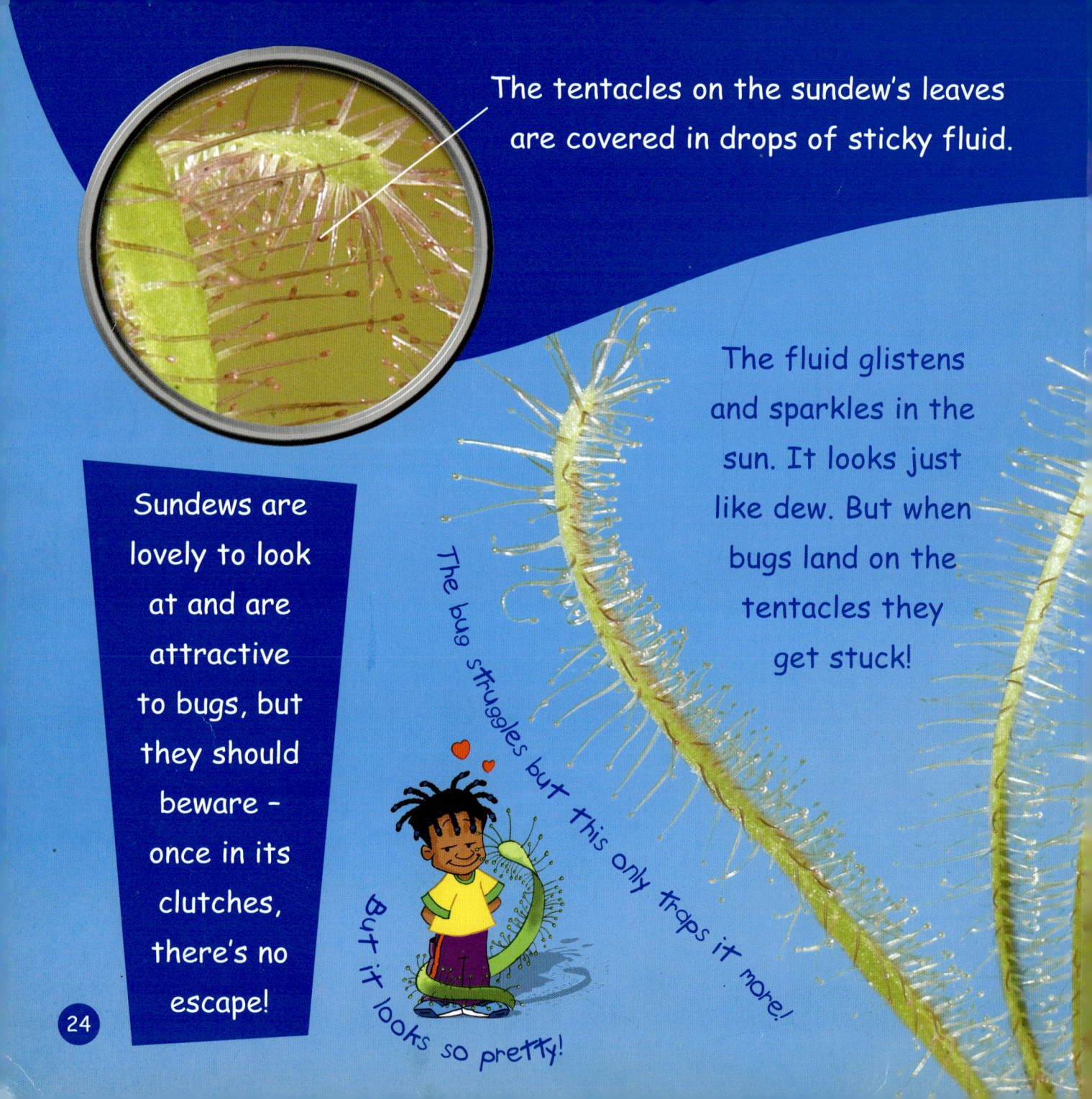

The tentacles on the sundew's leaves are covered in drops of sticky fluid.

The fluid glistens and sparkles in the sun. It looks just like dew. But when bugs land on the tentacles they get stuck!

Sundews are lovely to look at and are attractive to bugs, but they should beware – once in its clutches, there's no escape!

The bug struggles but this only traps it more!

But it looks so pretty!

it's a Sundew jungle

There are many different types of sundew. They can grow in very cold places like Siberia and very hot countries like Brazil.

The leaf curls around the bug...

...to make sure it can't escape.

The sundew releases proteins through its tentacles. These dissolve the trapped bug so the plant can absorb its goodness.

this is a butterwort

Can you see the tiny tentacles on the leaves?

The tentacles produce a gluey fluid. This makes the leaves feel like butter when you touch them.

Butterworts love to grow in mossy, mountainous places and boggy, wet places. Sometimes they even grow on trees.

Bugs are attracted to the beautiful flower.

▲ A butterwort's flower can be pink, violet or red.

26

The bug sticks to the fluid on the butterwort's leaves, like a fly sticks to flypaper! Then it is slowly dissolved and absorbed by the plant.

The leaves of the butterwort smell musty, a bit like mushrooms. This smell also attracts bugs.

This butterwort is from Ireland.

This is a bladderwort

The stem of the bladderwort can grow up to 3 metres high!

Bladderworts attract bugs with their flowers.

The trap is called a bladder. Each one is only about one millimetre wide.

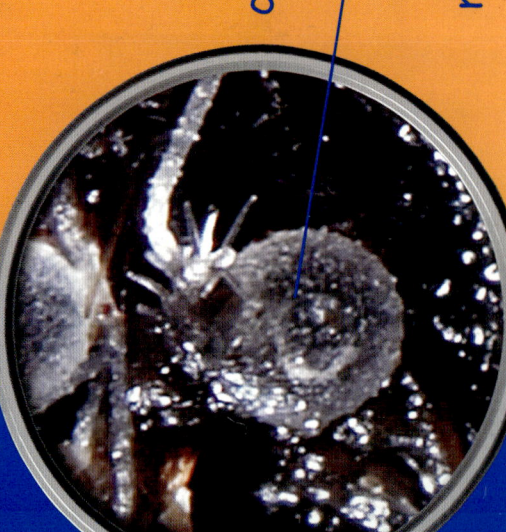

Bladderworts probably have the most complicated trap of all carnivorous plants – and possibly the tiniest. They are hidden, sometimes underground or underwater!

The bladder has a trap door which opens when a bug touches one of the two or three trigger hairs on the outside.

When a bug touches the trigger hairs, the bladder sucks them in like a vacuum cleaner, along with a small amount of water. The bladder then releases the water, but not the bug!

The traps are down here!

GLOSSARY

BACTERIA Group of tiny, microscopic organisms that live in soil, water or inside plants and animals. They cause chemical reactions that help plants and animals digest their food.

BOG An area of wet, spongy ground.

CARNIVORE A plant or animal that feeds on other animals.

DIGESTIVE JUICES Liquid inside an animal or plant that it uses to turn food into a form it can use.

HAIRS Thread-like growths on the surface of a plant or animal.

LEAVES Flat outgrowths on a plant's stems used to collect sunlight.

MICROSCOPIC Any object invisible to the naked eye.

NECTAR Sweet liquid produced by plants. It is collected by bees and made into honey.

ORGANISM Any animal or plant species.

PREY An animal caught by another animal or plant, as food.

PROTEIN Natural chemical found in plant and animal cells.

TEETH A hard, bony structure on a plant that resembles the teeth of animals.

TENTACLES Very long and very flexible parts of an animal or plant.

TRAPS Devices used by plants to catch insects.